©KYOKO WP 2022

BIG FEELS

To my daughters, who inspire me every single day. To Alex, for inspiring every single love poem. To the many hardships and life lessons that are the center of so many of these poems. To my best friends, for supporting me through them all. I love each and every one of you dearly. And to my late father, I will forever be your Kyokosan.

And to my cat, Theodore. For being cute.

Contents

Writing To Cope 21

More or Less 22

Open Book 23

My Words Can Be Musical 24

Big Pretty Words 22

Solace in my Rhyming 26

Always Enough 27

Measure of Worth 28

Deep Roots 29

Witching Hour 30

A Letter to Myself 31

Can't Find The Words 32

Every Ounce Completely 33

BIG FEELS

Little Yellow Flower 34
Eclipse 35
Do You Ever Stay Up At Night . . . 36
I Let My Crown Slip 37
From My Bedroom Window 38
Is Poetry Pretty? 39
My Soul Searching 40
Identity 41
Empath 42
True 43
Take Your Pain Away 44
Jess' Poem 45
Grief. 46
You Here With Me 47
Until it's Not 48
Our Love is Poetry 49

Dazzling Twinkle 50

Take My Hand and Never Let Go . 51

My Favorite Song 52

My Soul Awakening 53

My Home 54

Nothing Could be Better. 55

Don't Let Go 56

Sanctuary 57

Two Foxes. 58

Cradled in My Lovers Embrace . . . 59

Little Wildflowers. 60

You Save Me. 61

Have it All 62

My Darling 63

First Day 64

I Hope They Remember 65

For One Day 66

Clocks Tick, Clocks Tock 67

Stress 68

It's So Lonely To Be Ill 69

Palliative Care 70
Inside My Mind. 71
I Wish I Could Invite You In 72
My Emotions 73
A Sad Poem 74
Hard to Feel Sane 75
Watch Me As I Fall Apart 76
Dark Place 77
Most Days 78
Anxiety 79
Drowning 80
Edge of a Cliff 81
Why am I awake. 82
Pathless 83
Can You See Me? 84
How Ugly 85
Venomous 86

Broken Dam 87
Wrong With Me 88
Does it Make You Happy 89
Static 90
How Does It Feel 91
I Have No Say 92
Breaking 93
Bleeding Blue 94
To Feel Safe 95
PTSD 96
Blanket Fort 97
Footsteps and Heart Racing 98
Your Rage Kept Me In A Cage ... 99
4AM Never Late 100
Sleep Awaits 101
Deep Scar 102
Paralyzed 103

BIG FEELS

He Still Haunts Me 104
Ghost 105
Still 106
I Want to Sing, I Want to Fly. 107
Below The Surface. 108
Safe Grounding 109
I am Majestic 110
Thick Skin 111
Beautiful For Being Broken . . . 112
New Piece of Art. . . 113

Thank you!! …119

Bonus Special sneak peek at coming collection starts on page… 121

BIG FEELS

Writing to Cope

Writing to cope

        Coping to try

Trying to live

        Living to die

More or Less

The more I write

The less I cry

The less I want to die

The less I feel my lifes a lie

The more I write

The more I feel

The more I'm real

The more I don't have to conceal

The more I write

The less I drown,

The more I swim

The less I lose,

The more I find in a poem

Open Book

I'm an open book

Turn the page and take a look

Inside you'll find every emotion and feeling

The trauma and pain that still needs healing

The once frightened child

My thoughts gone wild

The tears that I've cried

All the times that I've tried

The love in my soul

Things I can't control

Every page, every chapter

Will have you wonder

How life hasn't snapped her

My Words Can Be Musical

Poetry is natural
I feel it in my soul,
It's almost spiritual
It's like a miracle,
When my thoughts can be lyrical,
Even though emotional
Come with rhythm and flow
They tumble, but roll
Every rhyme and riddle,
Has been instrumental
In a way, both healing and whimsical
My words, can be musical

Big Pretty Words

Anyone can find a few big pretty words and put them together but unless there is emotion and feeling behind them...

why bother?

If it doesn't come from the soul,

does it matter?

Solace in my Rhyming

It's hard to see everyone thriving
When you're barely surviving
Is my life reviving?
Or continually declining
As my pain is plotting, devising
Even disguising
Head first diving
I see no silver lining
I wish I could start rewinding
But also fast forward timing
For now I find solace in my rhyming
My words comprising
That's where my phoenix is rising

Never Too Much & Always Enough

You're never too much

And always enough

Remember these words when you want to give up

When you're feeling weak and things are tough

Life will be rough

Try to call your bluff

Just try not to sweat the small stuff

Sometimes you might have to go off the cuff

Let go of the clutch

Feel every little touch

Remember to make sure to fill your cup

And keep your chin up

You're never too much

And you're always enough

Measure of Worth

We measure our lives

By the trips we take around the sun

Never knowing when the ride will be done

So does it even matter to measure?

We measure our worth

By the things we acquire,

The money, our looks, our fashion attire

But we bare creativity and magic within

What if we measure our worth by our love, our art, our words, our kindness?

The things we do for others, the love we share, the moments of embrace

Every struggle we face

And come out of stronger

Wouldn't it be worth it to celebrate these moments longer?

You're worth more than a number.

More than your age, your money and looks

You are a soul first

And that soul's worth is priceless

It's a treasure that one cannot measure

Deep Roots

Nature entwined with my spirit

I feel its magic when I am near it

Deep roots connecting me to all that is natural

I feel its presence it's almost spiritual

The way the trees move my soul

Splendor growing out of control

A calming breeze moves around me

When surrounded by nature and all its beauty

The ground beneath me

The colors that I see

Majestic and moving gracefully

Watching the colors change fully

These roots are deep

The artistry can make me weep

Witching Hour

This is the time, for which I wait
It's dark and late
It's my favorite hour of the day
All is quiet, all is still;
It's delightful that way
I'm like a cat in the night.
I sit and I play,
With the thoughts in my head
All of the words left to be said
And they come at an ease
When I feel so at peace
All is calm, no one's awake
A pause on life; a break
I am grounded, like gravity
Finally, a moment of, clarity
In the ambient of darkness, the moon light shines, bounces, bends
I reflect and connect but soon this enchantment must come to an end

A Letter to Myself

Let go of all fears

Release the tension, the tears

Everything is not as it appears

Look in the mirror

You, yourself, have changed through the years

I've heard you sing with my ears

Don't you see dear?

It may not seem clear

But absolutely nothing about you is meer

Good things are near

Can't Find the Words

Can't find the words to say
But I have a song in my heart,
That I don't know how to convey
I've known love and I've been broken apart
But I can't find the words today to make into art

Every Ounce Completely

Her soul is so full,

She cannot control

That it pours from her eyes

That's why she cries

She feels everything all the time

That is something she cannot hide

Emotions written on her face,

Heart on her sleeve,

Her feelings are not lies

She feels it all deeply

Every ounce completely

Some say she's blessed

Some say she's cursed

But apathy would be so much worse

Instead of sinking, she swims in her emotion

With each and every wave that comes from that ocean.

Little Yellow Flower

How can one feel the need

To say a dandelion is just a weed?

It's planted

Enchanted

Wish granted

To say it's a weed is simply tragic

Dandelions are truly magic

From little yellow flower

To puff spreading its power

It's planted

Enchanted

Wish granted

Be it a weed or not

The charmed dandelion must not be forgot

Eclipse

She was like an eclipse

Never could quite catch a glimpse

Glimpse of her soul, her heart, her mind

How someone so broken and beaten could still be so kind

She pretends to be fine

She was like an eclipse

Never could quite catch a glimpse

Do You Ever Stay Up At Night?

Do you ever stay up at night?
Going over every detail;
Everything that wasn't right
Do you ever stay up at night?
Staring at the clock
Mind still putting up a fight
Do you ever stay up at night?
Stressing and obsessing until morning light
Do you ever stay up at night?

I Let My Crown Slip

I let my crown slip

I lost my grip

Fell from my pedestal

Made myself look a fool

I feel the way you see me now

Knowing I'll never again be worthy of your bow

No longer deserving

You only see in me what is vile and self serving is

I've lost my nobility

And with that my ability

To have you

I let my crown slip

From My Bedroom Window

Hear the soothing music of the birds so free

As they sing on swaying branches of my favorite tree

Watch as the leaves are dancing gracefully

To the songs that they sing so effortlessly

Feel the gentle, flowing breeze

As it passes through the changing leaves

And taste autumns season, swiftly approaching

Is Poetry Pretty?

Is Poetry pretty?

I don't know if that's always true

I guess it all depends on what the words do

How you place them and which ones you choose

Do they describe and illuminate?

Are they raw? Can they relate?

There is beauty in tragedy

And I guess that's what I have in me

And makes up most of my poetry

So, maybe, Poetry *is* pretty

My Soul Searching

Born in this world alone and naked

Cold, shaking, afraid

Longing for only one thing since birth

Forever trying to prove my worth

My soul to feel another

To feel love at last

My soul needs to be flooded

My soul held, beheld, beloved

Identity

I've always struggled between two races

I look in the mirror and see two faces

Too Asian to be white

Too white to be Asian

Where do I fit in this equation?

I always wanted to just be one

No more confusion inside of me

No more questioning my own identity

No guesses or questions of "what are you?"

I am just me but I feel split in two

I can't seem to find my place in society

And it may fill me with anxiety

But I know regardless, I am mighty

Empath

Part of feeling too much
Is the ability to feel the touch
The touch of deep emotion in everything
Which at times can be a blessing
You can even pull each emotion apart
And turn it into a piece of art
The curse is how deep the pain can feel
And living in it like you're a slow reel
Every ache and pain
On replay, the same
Part of feeling too much is the ability to feel the touch
The touch of every wave of emotion
Swimming, sinking or drowning within this ocean

True

If "what doesn't kill you makes you stronger" is true

Then where are my muscles of honor?

I'm long over due

If pressure makes coal into diamonds

Why aren't I dazzling? Shiny? Or new?

They said "it can't rain forever"

But they've never experienced this weather

Must not live where I do If "tough times don't last but tough people do"

Then why do I feel like I'm constantly coming unglued

They say, "just keep swimming"

And I always do

As long as I'm living

My heart will stay true

Take Your Pain Away

If I could take it away I would
 I would rather take the blow for you
Than for you to know the pain too
I would take every ounce of hurt away
Keep it in my own heart to stay
I would rather that than see you break
That's why all your pain I wish to take

Jess' Poem

I hate to see you in such pain

I see you struggle to contain

Like you're paralyzed in the pouring rain

You can let it out, cry; your eyes don't have to strain

I know you think you have to maintain

Even though you've been hit by a train

Give yourself permission to breathe;

To take it in, pause and refrain

Grief

Missing you comes in waves and sometimes
It's hard not to slip under the current of grief
There's nothing to hold onto.
No rope, no rescue, no return, no relief
Feel like I'm sinking in the endless deep
Drowning in the tears I weep

You Here With Me

I still remember the day you died

My brain didn't believe it...

It denied and denied

I spent weeks, months, years …

Crying for you

I wanted everyone to say they were lying;

that it wasn't true

But you're still not here..You're really gone

It doesn't seem fair;

I didn't have you that long

Since you've been gone

I've felt so alone

Nowhere to go, to run to, to call home

I see you in my dreams all the time

And even though I know it's not real and that you're not alive

I still try to keep the dreams going forever in my mind

I wish you were here but I know that can't be

But I selfishly long for it...You here with me

Until it's Not

A rock is just a rock until it's not

Not when it's something saw and thought,

"This is beautiful and shall not be forgot."

Our Love is Poetry

You are my One

My only

The one I want

Forever to hold me

The one whose scent I find so sweetly

The only one

To know me deeply

The one to love me

Utterly and completely

The one I want forever

For us to become we

The one who is my He

And I, his She

Our love is Poetry

Dazzling Twinkle

My soul longed for you before my eyes even saw you
Dazzling twinkle getting brighter
Finally, my eyes recognized what my soul already knew

Take My Hand and Never Let Go

I know we said we'd take it slow

But won't you take my hand and never let go

Love, look me in the eyes

When I tell you no lies

There will be no bidding goodbyes

For forever with you is where my heart resides

You're everything to me, my feelings I can't disguise

You've made my love grow infinite in size

I can't emphasize

So take my hand and never let go

And I'll do my best to lift you when you're feeling low

My Favorite Song

I listen on repeat
It's the only thing I want to hear
Such a beautiful melody
Calming notes eliminate fear
I could never tire of this song
It's familiar; it's been there all along
Every heart has a song but yours is the only one,
I'm listening to
Every heart has a song and mine belongs,
To only you

My Soul Awakening

The moment it happened
I was neither scared nor shaking
I was at ease
My heart for the taking
No more delaying
My soul awakening

My Home

My home is warm

My home is safe

It's cozy and comfy

And cannot be replaced

My favorite scent; I can only smell there

It fills me glee

Makes my heart happy; a smile I can taste

So overwhelmed with love and peace

It calms my heart and slows down its pace

I wish I could take my home everywhere or never leave

But that isn't the case

Because my home is a person

A heart, soul and body

My home has a face

My home is love

My home is warm

My home is safe

Nothing Could be Better

It's raining

It's pouring

But with you it's never boring

Cuddled Up

Cozy and warm

Laughter louder than the storm

Your hands are soft

As they hold mine

Nowhere I'd rather be in space or time

In this moment nothing is wrong

Everything is right like a perfect love song

I listen to the sound of your heart beat

As I lay my head on your chest

Nothing could be better

Because this is the best

You move my hair

And kiss my forehead

And my heart could not be happier than lying with you in bed

I squeeze you tight

Overwhelmed with love

There isn't anything I'd rather be doing that I can think of

Don't Let Go

If I fall, would you catch me?

If I faint, would you save me?

I'm falling deep and feeling breathless

The waves of pain are so relentless

Hold on now, don't let go, don't regret this

There may be waves of pain

But my love for you,

Is endless

Sanctuary

All things are temporary

Even if it feels contrary

To have a lot to carry

A lot of pain to bury

It can be quite scary

To feel like you can function barely

It's understandable to be reactionary

But you weren't made to be ordinary

You were made to be evolutionary

And that is honorary

Your life will be legendary

Even when it hurts momentarily

Your life should be your primary

You're such a visionary

And that's not imaginary

Because you are pure luminary

And I'll be your sanctuary

Two Foxes

There once was a fox so lonely and sad
This fox didn't know how bad it she had
.

A fox so scared
A fox so meek
A fox didn't look
A fox didn't seek

There once was fox roaming through life
He buried his feelings, his pain his strife

A fox so sly
A fox so mystique
A fox didn't look
A fox didn't seek

There once was a day when sun broke through the trees
The foxes, not seeking, could finally see.
He saw her eyes and She felt his strength
Soon the distance between them; less than an arm's length
Two foxes together are better than one
Two foxes can play; two foxes can run
Two foxes no longer alone on their own
Two foxes together finally found their home

There was once were two foxes

Cradled in My Lovers Embrace

The chaos is calm
The loud noise silenced
Heart rate is steady
Surrounded by warmth
Cradled in my lovers embrace
I can breathe; I am safe

Little Wildflowers

Little wild flowers

Each strong and vibrant in their own way

Sprouted from the ground

Each to bloom their own day

Little wildflowers

Different colors and shapes,

Such a marvelous bouquet

Dance with the flowing breeze,

Like a graceful ballet

Little wildflowers

You look so lovely today

BIG FEELS

You Save Me

You saved my life
Before you were born
I was no longer thinking of me
Everything was you
My entire universe, the sun, the moon
Kicking in my belly to your favorite tune
Hearing me sing from within the womb
You saved my life
When you were born
So was a place I didn't know existed, deep in my heart
A life worth living for, this is the start
Embracing my new role in life, my new part
My love for you is nothing short of poetic art
You saved my life
I'm so glad you were born
You taught me to love and be loved in return
Every lesson for you was one I also had to learn
You make my heart yearn for every smile I earn
You save my life now
You saved my life then
You saved my life everyday from beginning to end
This love is magic, it's not pretend
It's the purest form, none could contend
You've saved my life
Because on mine, you depend

Have it All

Giggles and laughs
And sweet baby baths
Cooing and crawling
Walking and falling
Growing everyday and finding their voice
Making sure that every time they make the choice
Temper tantrums and many tears
Learning every day and finding out fears
From in your arms to holding hands
Playing with barbies, no more pots and pans
Getting bigger and going to school
I hope they still think I'm cool
Seasons change and school years pass
You'll never believe how it happens so fast
One day you're swaddling your newborn tight
And the next they're in high school shining so bright
But no matter how big and no matter how small
You will always love them and want them to have it all

My Darling

Sparkle in eyes

Joy glistens like the sunrise

Light as a feather and float like one too

Sweetness is that of fresh honeydew

Pure heart, beaming innocence

I hope to always remember you like this

Little girl

My pearl

My whole world

First Day

Raindrops

At bus stops

The sun, still lights the sky

Hugs and kisses little bird,

Go fly

I Hope They Remember

I hope they remember before mom was sick

Mom loved to play and mom wasn't stuck in bed all day

I hope they remember before mom was sick

When she was healthy and strong and nothing stood in her way

I hope they remember before mom was sick

When mom could take them out and about, when mom didn't pass out

I hope they remember before mom was sick

Smiles on faces and fun happy places

I hope they remember before mom was sick

When she smothered them with love and wasn't stuck in her bedroom, one floor above

I hope they remember before mom was sick

Mom was the one; mom was the only one who could get anything done

I hope they remember before mom was sick

Before doctors appointments and hospital visits

She wanted to do everything right, she didn't want to quit

And tried hard every single day to keep up with it

She never intended to be living like this

I hope they remember before mom was sick

For One Day

Just for one day

I'd like to wake up full of life

To feel rested through my whole body

To feel refreshing energy

Just for one day

I'd like a steady heart

To feel the calming rhythmic beats

To feel its soothing melody as I breathe

Just for one day

I'd like to run in fields of flowers

To feel the breeze as I frolic through the trees

To feel free

Just for one day

I'd like my body to be copacetic

To feel the simplicity,

I just can't obtain; the mundane

To feel no pain

I'd like to feel okay

Even if only,

Just for one day

Clocks Tick, Clocks Tock

Clocks tick

As I sit

Waiting for the doctors to tell me I'm sick

I'm tired of waiting for this

Every appointment a new diagnosis

A new plan of action on how to approach it

Another referral, new doctor visit

The anxiety deep in my stomach, the pit

I'm so sick of being sick

I still sit

Clocks tick, clocks tock

My heart pounds,

I hear the door as they knock

What will it be today, Doc?

Stress

They say stay away from triggers that increase the symptoms; like stress

But I don't know how to do that when my whole life feels a mess

It only makes me feel sicker

And then my problems; bigger

I get stuck in a cycle I can't seem to quit

The pain, no sleep, nausea, vomit

Fatigue, muscles cramping, headaches, all of it

Bound in this go round, I want off of it

They say stay away from triggers that increase the symptoms; like stress

This is my life with chronic illness

It's So Lonely To Be Ill

Doctors and pills

Therapists and goodwill

Procedures and blood draws

Operations and white gauze

Tear drops and can't sleep

Fresh wounds skin deep

It's lonely to be ill

Self love? Self care? Self what? Who? Where?

The sunshine, the yoga

The essential oils of Aunt Rhoda

The diets and deep breathing

But I'm still here dry heaving

No meditation or willingness

Can take away the illness

It's so lonely to be ill

Hospital stays and beeping nights

When am I ever going to feel right?

More prods more pokes

More pain it invokes

Don't forget to take your meds

Enjoy your day alone in bed

It's so lonely to be ill

Palliative Care

Palliative care

The words so hard to digest

I just think of death

And what will I do with the rest

Of life I have left

Doesn't always mean death

But it still hurts in the depth

Of my soul, can't quite catch my breath

Like my lungs are compressed

The words keep playing, my brain obsessed

They're hard to digest

As I previously confessed

But they won't put me to rest

I have no bullet proof vest

But I still have dreams and

Wishes filled in my hope chest

Inside My Mind

Inside my mind

It's not always kind

Just like the outside drowning under the tide

My mind can be a very dark place

A warm, loving, sad, lonely, dark place

I Wish I Could Invite You In

I wish I could invite you in but I'm afraid it's such a mess

So many things have piled up; causing abundant stress

I wish I could invite you in but I'm afraid I'm too embarrassed

To show you all that I hide inside; the disarray at my barest

I wish I could invite you in but I'm afraid I'm quite ashamed

The catastrophe in the interior

The chaos that needs tamed

I wish I could invite you in

My Emotions

I hate my emotions

So many tears I could fill an ocean

I have to keep my brain in motion

Or I fear a mental explosion

There's so much pain and commotion

I wish there was a magic potion

I don't know why I was chosen

I see no sun I am broken

Heart ripped open

Needs to be woven

No serotonin

I hate my emotions

A Sad Poem

Feel hopeless and empty

I'm having a sad

I've cried tears of plenty

But don't feel so bad

My heart is aching

Breaking a tad

My thoughts are shaking I must be mad

But worry for me none

I'm just having a sad

It's not even the saddest one that I've had

Hard to Feel Sane

It's hard to feel sane

When you can't trust your own brain

That's the refrain

And the refrain is always the same

It's hard to feel sane

Watch Me As I Fall Apart

Watch Me as I Fall Apart

Right now just existing hurts so bad

Put me in a coma and wake me when its over

There's nothing I can do when I feel so sad

I don't want to be awake I'm losing my composure

Feelings overwhelm my soul, thoughts overwhelm my body

The sadness that's inside of me is starting to consume me

I'm crying tears that could fill rooms and feeling very empty

There's nowhere to run or hide...

So, everyone can see

Watch me as I fall apart

Watch me as I crumble

The pieces that once made my heart

Are now nothing more than rubble

I'm sinking deeper into the dark

The waves of sadness going over my head

The terrible journey I've had to embark

Battling thoughts of wishing I was dead

Dark Place

I'm not in a good head space
I'm in a really dark place
Don't want to look at my face
All I see is disgrace
Feeling like I'm just a waste
Longing for a warm embrace
Searching for a familiar face
Something to help in anyway
Do I not deserve grace?
To feel safe
It's not the case
For now, I'll cry in my dismay
My life in disarray
Will I make another day?

Most Days

Most days I don't get out of bed
I just try to escape the thoughts in my head
I'm drowning while everyone lives their lives
I'm home watching the latest Housewives
I'm under my covers safe at home
But I just wish one thing, that I wasn't alone
I just try to escape the thoughts in my head
Most days I don't get out of bed

Anxiety

Dig dig

Bleed bleed

I can't fight the need

Ripping skin until it's done

Blood is dripping from my thumb

Dig dig

Bleed bleed

This is my anxiety

Drowning

Slipping under deep waves
Feel the waters harsh embrace
The sea rarely ever behaves
Can't swim, can't keep pace
Drowning; blue in the face
I think I'm losing this race
My lungs concave

Edge of a Cliff

Feel like I'm on the edge of a cliff
This is certainly no way to live
It's not that I want to die
I just don't want to hurt and cry

Why Am I Awake

Why am I awake?
I want to sleep
And yet here I am
Sitting in bed as I weep
Something robbing
Me, I can't control
And I am sobbing
Cant console
I want to rest
I want to dream
I hold my breath
Try not to scream
My brain is wired
My emotions, on fire
My body, tired
Why am I awake?

Pathless

It's hard to avoid the sadness

When you're surrounded by constant madness

All of the ugly and the badness

It puts me at a disadvantage

It's hard to see the light in pitch blackness

I think of what life would be like if I didn't have this

Would it just be plain and blandness?

For now I'm still finding my way out of the vastness

Wish I could take the trauma; compact it

My brain likes to replay; reenact it

Every moment in exactness

Just trying to get past this

Make my pain past tense

But I often feel pathless

Can You See Me?

Am I invisible?

Can you see me?

Is this not the ground beneath me?

Can you not see what I see?

Sometimes even I wonder, "Who is she?"

I'm trapped in time, what'll it take to break free?

Is this how it's going to be?

There has to be a key

That can connect me

Back to some degree

Of reality

How Ugly

My worst critic

My harshest judge

Everything I did, every face I made

Filled you with disgust

As would anything I would touch

And you never missed a chance to make sure I knew I wasn't enough

You campaigned against me

Filled with nothing but hate

You should've been my support

But never took the time to relate

I was your personal punching bag

Your outlet for anger

You could not have cared less if I was in danger

I looked up to you

But you only looked down upon me

Because you could never take a moment to try to see

How these things affected me

Made me hate my own identity

And are forever instilled in my memory

I will never forget how ugly

Venomous

I'm feeling quite tremulous

The pain in my heart is strenuous

I fear it may be continuous

It's where my hurt has made a venue of

It's shattered quite tremendous

I don't know if I can live with this

Something spreading; venomous

I'm feeling breathlessness

Just endless

Helplessness

Where there once was

Preciousness

And I am weaponless

Broken Dam

It takes just one tear to form and drop

Once they start the floodgates are open

The deteriorating dam holding them back is broken

Nothing I can do now to make it stop

Wrong With Me

Sometimes I wonder what it is that's wrong with me

And if I'll ever become who I once had the potential to be

I often wonder if my flaws are all you see

Because all I see is what's wrong with me

Am I not worthy?

Can I be happy?

Does it Make You Happy

Do you enjoy making me cry?

With every tear that drops from my eyes?

Does it make you feel so happy?

Does it fill you with glee to see me in misery?

Is the only thing holding us together, a history?

Well, "if it makes you happy, it can't be that bad"....

I don't know if that's what she meant but I'm pretty sure that's what she said

I Have No Say

I have no say
I have no say what happens to me
I'm silent, submissive and always agree
I have a few friends who to try to hang out
They travel to see me;
They take a long route
Sometimes on their way they run into trouble
It hurts my insides I can feel the blood bubble
And Sometimes I have guests I didn't invite
But it doesn't matter
I can't put up a fight
They violate me; I yell I shout
I want them to leave; they won't get out
When the pain is too bad; unwanted guests won't leave
And I have no control; I cry and I grieve
I say enough is Enough
I say no more, the highways too rough
I'm screaming but no one can hear me
I have no rights; I just want to be free
But I have no voice I have no choice
I have no say

Static

My brain is so noisy today
Can't understand what it's trying to say
Too much sound it doesn't make sense
What am I supposed to do with this?
Its deafening static

How Does It Feel

Waking up crying
Feeling empty in my heart
We were so connected
Now we feel two worlds apart
A pain in the gut I can't ignore
Tell me, how does it feel to not love me anymore?

Breaking

Heart aching

Tears streaming

Body shaking

Inside screaming

I am breaking

Bleeding Blue

It hurts when you can feel some one stop loving you

And there's absolutely nothing you can do

But you know in your heart what's true

And you wish you could undo

What happened, too

But your heart is just left bleeding blue

To Feel Safe

I want to feel safe.
I want to feel secure.
I'm riding this roller coaster,
It's hard to endure.
I need some stability, something concrete.
Something that makes my soul feel complete.
Something that tethers me, like gravity to my feet.
I need to feel safe.

PTSD

For many, forgotten feelings flee
But mine are always a part of me
They come in the form of **PTSD**
I don't forget, nor does my body
Forever, they are a part of me

Blanket Fort

The chaos inside

I just want to hide

From the world and myself

Close the book

Put it on a shelf

Hide under the covers

Until the chaos calms and I feel safe

A blanket fort is my closest escape

Footsteps and Heart Racing

Footsteps and heart racing

The fear I feel when I hear him pacing

He's angry, he's mad, he's looking for me

I'm hiding; I'm crying and hoping he won't see

He finds me, I'm naked, alone and I scream

He grabs me and drags me

He screams words, so cruel so obscene

I cry, I beg and I pray

But he throws me around and

Now the grounds where I lay

I try to stay still until I know its all clear

While he sits grumbling in his chair drinking his beer

Your Rage Kept Me In A Cage

You kept me in a cage; chained and locked.
There was no way out that was not blocked.
Kidnapped. Wings strapped. Completely Trapped.
Days go by. I still don't fly.
Hope decreased.
Would I ever be released?
I won't let him keep me here.
I won't be controlled by fear.
It's time things are changing.
It's time to break free from the caging.
I fought and felt stripped from the chains that I ripped.
My wings for so long held down and gripped
But they could not possibly ever be clipped
I was once in your prison.
But from those dwellings, I have finally risen.

4am Never Late

Dry heaving

Heavy breathing

Heart pounding

Can't find grounding

4am; never late

160 heart rate

Hands shake

I don't want to be awake

But I don't want to be asleep

The trauma simply runs too deep

Nightmares

And jump scares

Torture and terror

Heartbreak and despair

Lives lived in dreams

Tears shed, loud screams

Wake up sweating

Drenched my bedding

4am; never late

160 heart rate

I don't want to be awake

Sleep Awaits

Goodnight moon

Goodnight stars

Goodnight pain

And goodnight scars

Sleep awaits

My tortured fate

I can't escape

This evening date

Wicked nightmares

Horrifying layers

Though, they may not be real

It does not change, how they feel

I wonder, will I ever heal

Deep Scar

You really went too far

You really left the wounds raw

Damage spoken

Bashed and broken

Cut and open

Skin exposin'

You really went too far

You really left a deep scar

Paralyzed

Do you ever feel like you're paralyzed in time?

Frozen in a moment,

Life is still moving around you

But you can't feel the ground beneath you

And you can't seem to find

Anything to hold on to

To fast forward or rewind

So, you're trapped in a place with no clear escape

Stuck in the feeling of fight or flight

Can't trust your own mind to know day from night

The world you once knew is still collapsing

While you sit there still trying to fill gaps in

From moments lost and time taken

While you got through life constantly faking

Faking the smile that you've moved on and healed

While underneath the trauma and pain are concealed

Still paralyzed in time

But on the exterior, appearing fine

He Still Haunts Me

He still haunts me

He can live he can be free

But I am still frozen

Because he still haunts me

He can move on he can forget what he did to me

But I am still frozen

Because he still haunts me

He can run, and jump through life with ease

But I am still frozen

Because he still haunts me

Years have passed and the time has gone swiftly

But I am still frozen

Because he still haunts me

Ghost

You're just a ghost

But I still feel you

You're just a ghost

But I still feel you

I feel you in every panic attack

I feel you when my heart races

I feel you in every palpitation

I feel you when my brain paces

When I'm spiraling out of control

Your ghost surrounds me

And when I'm crying tears that no one can console

Your ghost surrounds me

You're just a ghost

But I still feel you

I feel you in every tear

I feel you in every place

I feel you in every fear

I feel you in everything that awaits

When I'm losing my breath

Your ghost surrounds me

When it feels like the only answer is death

Your ghost surrounds me

You're just a ghost

But I still feel you

Still

The pain in my skin

I still feel it

The sound of his voice

I still hear it

The cigarettes and alcohol

I can still taste it

The panic inside

I still drown in it

I close my eyes

I still see you

What will it take to heal and rid you?

I Want to Sing, I Want to Fly

A bird is free to fly and roam

A bird can make anywhere their home

I hope to be a bird one day

But for now locked and caged I stay

The birds they sing with joy and freedom

I have no voice, I cannot greet them

I sit alone trapped with out hope

If a bird cannot sing then how can it cope?

The days go by and still I am silent

I spend all of my days just keeping quiet

I want to sing, I want to fly

I want to be way up high in the sky

Singing my song to all that can hear

This is my dream, despite what I fear

One day I'll make it

One day I'll sing

One day I'll feel the wind under each wing

BIG FEELS

Below The Surface

He thought he had me in his hands.
Convinced me of his lies
It was all a part of his plans
Filled my head with doubt and deceit
I had nowhere to go but down to dwell in defeat
Slipping away, sinking fast.
Powerless to the spell he cast
Struggling to stay above the surface
I watched my life fade away
I felt no purpose
Falling into the deep dark
My light diminishing
Heart beat fading, gasping for air
Below the surface,
It was there, you found me
Drowning in the depths of darkness
Your light surrounds me
Slipping away, sinking fast
You came to save me at last
Slipping away, sinking fast
I knew you'd save me at last

Safe Grounding

I'm falling faster; deeper into the abyss
Thinking about all the time I might miss
The gravity, the force; increasing pressure
The distance from here to the ground I can't measure
Increasing Heart rate, I can feel it pounding
I don't want to die I just need safe grounding

I am Majestic

I lived in hell for many years

Living in a constant state of panic and fear

Increasing every time the devil drew near

He drew more power with every tear

Questioning my thoughts, made my own memories disappear

I didn't even recognize myself in the mirror

Until I found my strength, my spear

Now his screams I can't even hear

He has no power, and I have no fear

I am majestic and he is mere

Thick Skin

They say I need thick skin
That I am too weak
But I've been through plenty
Maybe this is where I peak
They tell me I need to get tough.
I tell them I just feel too much
You don't need thick skin
You don't need to be strong
It's okay if you're sad and cry all day long
It's okay not to be okay
No matter what they might say
I know what I am and need to be
But wearing my heart on my sleeve
Is a part of me
I don't need thick skin
I'm just a body with a sensitive soul within

More Beautiful For Being Broken

I am more beautiful for being broken

I am making myself whole again

The shards; the cracks

Every piece; I've picked up

I am the one who put those pieces back

I am the one to put myself together again

I am more beautiful for being broken

Piece of Art
(Kintsukuroi)

Every word is a memory
Each a punch in the gut,
a crack in the heart.
But these wounds
somehow craft me
into a new piece of art.

BIG FEELS

I write for me, as therapy

If you feel it too, I write for you

BIG FEELS

A Little Extra Poem

The Morning Wait

It's peaceful

It's calm

But she is not

But for a few short moments

The chaos is forgot

We wait while the sun rises

Peeking from the cloud disguises

The world is still

Birds still sleeping

Leaves move slowly with the breeze

The morning wait puts my soul at ease

BIG FEELS

Thank you to everyone reading this book. I hope you now feel a little less alone in your thoughts and with your feelings. I hope it inspires you!

And if you love writing remember,

If it comes from soul and from your heart,
Then it is beautiful and it is art.

Much Love,
Kyoko W.P.

BIG FEELS

SNEAK PEEK of collection to come…

The Wrong One

No matter what you will always find fault
Fault in anything I do or have done
You never once give me the benefit of doubt
You've already decided I was the wrong one
Kyoko W.P.

Losing you

The decisions been made
It's very clear
Lay me down in my grave
You won't shed one tear
Leave me here, afraid
Because losing you *is my biggest fear*
Kyoko W.P.

The Prelude

Been beaten and bruised
Blamed and accused
Turned away and refused
Felt empty and used
Lost and confused
Utterly disapproved
But allow me to be excused
I'm no longer consumed
That was just the *prelude*
Because I have cocooned
Through metamorphosis,
I have been improved
Remewed
      Kyoko W.P.

Golden Dust

All in a golden afternoon, under the skies of cloudless blue
I see your face, feel your warmth & reach out to you
Eyes are sparkling from the sun shining down
There's an enchanting sparkle, glistening, all around
Enriched with magnificent golden dust
Natures beauty surrounding us

Kyoko W.P.

BIG FEELS

Bad Dream

Chaos and cancer
War and disaster
Make it go faster
Feel frozen in a bad dream
Is everything as bad as it seems?
What does any of this even mean?
I don't know, but it's breaking my heart
Come take a look,
it's falling apart

Kyoko W.P.

With Gold

I am, but a sensitive soul
Living in a world of fear and control
Feeling every motion push and pull
Lately, it feels, it's taken a toll
I can feel myself start to unravel; unroll
But I won't grow cold
Oh, no

My cracks are filled with gold

Kyoko W.P.

Your Souls Engraving

I've always craved a sense of belonging,
Never felt I was one to fit in
Always trying, always fawning
But then I met you, goose bumps on my skin
It was you I had been craving,
It is you, whom I belong
Your souls engraving,
On my Soul, like a melodic love song
Kyoko W.P.

Tender Love

Your love is something new,
So tender
My body had no choice but to completely surrender
Itself
To You
It's like nothing in my life
I've ever felt
So I'll stay here in this moment
And melt
Away
With you

Kyoko W.P,

Anxious

I can't even take this
I don't have the patience
I'm nervous and anxious
My chest feels tight where it once felt spacious

Kyoko W.P.

Rhythm and Rhyme

Poetry speaks to me
In a way so eloquently
The words paint what you can't see
As they pour out of my memory
A masterpiece in the making
There will be no regret or forsaking
In my rhythm & rhyme making
Because to me,
it's breathtaking

Kyoko W.P.

BIG FEELS

Made in the USA
Columbia, SC
03 May 2023

16003774R00070